*For young girls who have.....*

*The Dream*

*The Goal*

*The Determination*

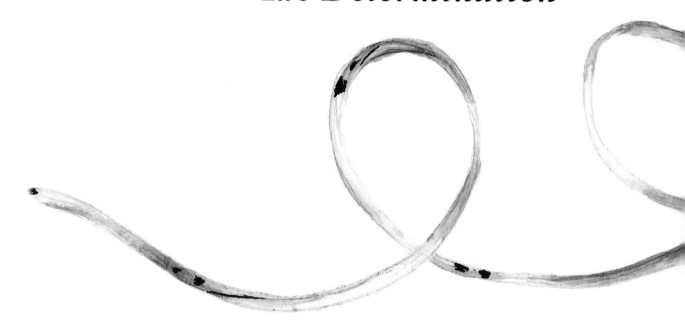

With a hoop, ribbon, ball, rope and clubs,
an aspiring young athlete finds her place in
the world of Rhythmic Gymnastics.

# NATALI'S

## THE TRUE STORY OF A

A modern day ugly duckling, Natali finds herself frustrated with gymnastics until she discovers rhythmic gymnastics. Once she finds a sport that highlights her strengths, she thrives and accomplishes more than she had ever imagined. Her determination and training allow her to overcome her

WRITTEN & ILLUSTRATED BY
### FRAN VICTOR

# JOURNEY

## RHYTHMIC GYMNAST

fears and finally succeed, changing her life forever. This book is based on a true story about my daughter who began rhythmic gymnastics at age eight and went on to win the Junior Olympic National Championship in 2001 at age 12.

Design & Layout by Carlos Fraga
carlos@directdevelopment.com

Natali was an active little girl right from the start. She was always jumping and tumbling on the furniture, riding her tricycle, climbing on the monkey bars or her play structure. When she was 3, she cartwheeled along the sand at the beach while her family stood by amazed.

Just happened to be the start of school and the start of after school gymnastics classes. Some of the kids were going and asked Natali to come along and try it.

Well, she did and it was a perfect fit. Natali was very happy to be at the gym. She worked hard, trying to improve.

2

Natali took a deep breath. She had been preparing for this all year. It was tryouts for the gymnastics team and the back handspring was required to make the team.

"I know I can do this," she thought, even though she had fallen several times. Jill, her coach, was very patient but was beginning to have doubts. Everyone looked concerned. Natali tried many times. Although she never cried, tears were building in her eyes.

4

"What's happening?" she thought. All the girls were able to do it. Natali looked at herself. She was tall, lean and flexible, not sturdy like her teammates. One girl offered to help her. "Watch me," she said, as she bolted backwards across the floor.

"What's wrong with me," Natali thought. Her concerns grew as she heard one of her teammates whisper, "She's not like us, she won't make it."

Jill called for the girls to line up for team tryouts. Natali's turn came. She tried her hardest but fell once more. As she walked off the floor, she knew she didn't make the team.

While Natali sat teary eyed, her coach came over and sat next to her. Natali imagined the worst; Jill would ask her to quit. Instead, Jill put her arm around her and asked, "Have you ever watched the Rhythmic Gymnasts?" "No, what's that?" Natali asked. Her coach pointed far across the crowded floor to another team, a smaller team of gymnasts who were practicing.

They were conditioned, strong and very coordinated, tossing spectacular throws in the air with their balls and catching them gently in the palm of their hands with control and precision. Natali handled the ball which she found out is weighted and made of plastic.

Natali liked the equipment.

She and her parents met with the rhythmic coach, Tina, who had been watching Natali for some time, noticing that her body type and flexibility might be a good fit for rhythmic gymnastics. Natali decided to try it.

Stretching is important. Rhythmic gymnasts are known for extreme maneuvers in their routines.

Tina helped Natali with stretching.
She progressed quickly. It helped that she
was born with natural flexibility.

Conditioning and strengthening are essential, allowing difficult maneuvers to appear effortless.

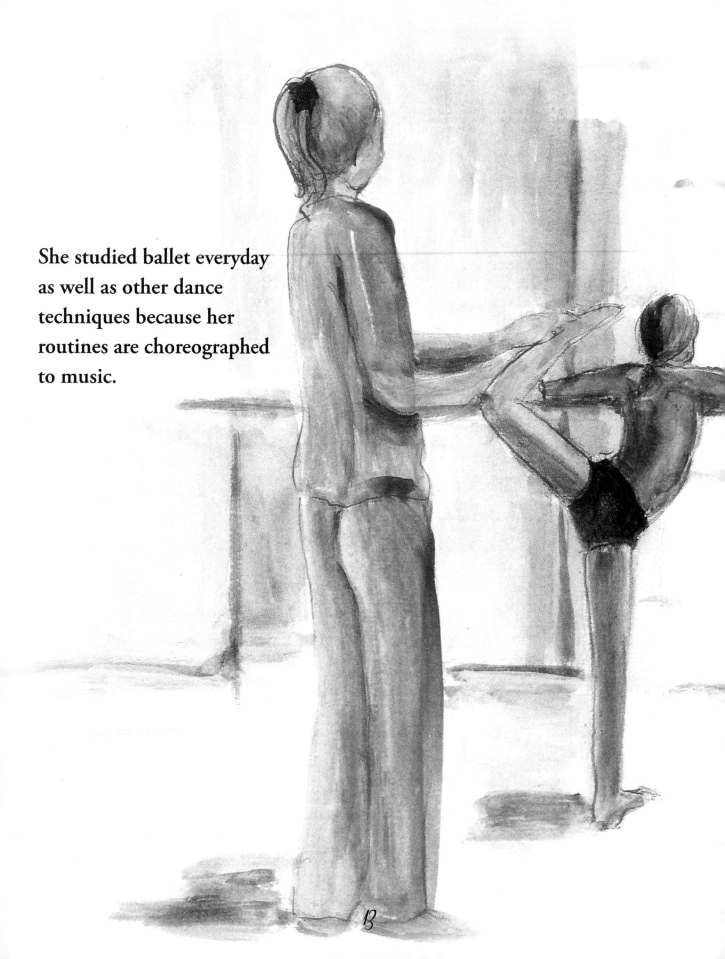

She studied ballet everyday as well as other dance techniques because her routines are choreographed to music.

This helped her develop grace and expressive form while carrying out flexibility maneuvers with strength, coordination, confidence and poise.

Natali started with basic compulsory floor exercises, unique to the lower levels. In compulsory routines, rhythmic gymnasts practice and perfect elements while performing the same skills to the same music.

15

She did leaps, turns, jumps and flexibility moves.
Natali's ballet and music training were helpful.

There are five types
of equipment in
rhythmic gymnastics:

balls

clubs

ropes

hoops

and ribbons.

Tina introduced Natali to all of them and
everyone was patient. It was difficult but fun
to learn the unique skills that are needed to
perform with each piece of equipment.

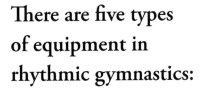

The rope is usually made of hemp with knots at the ends and cut to Natali's height. She was taught to create winding, serpent-like figures with it while remaining agile and elegant.

Incorporating flexibility and strength with pointed toes and a straight leg make this an advanced maneuver with the rope.

The ribbon is silk, 6.5 yards long with a stick attached. It may look easy as it moves, but it is very difficult to maneuver. Long and light, it may be thrown in different directions to create designs in space, making images and shapes of every kind.

While sometimes leaping and jumping, snakes, spirals and throws are essentials of the ribbons flight.

20

The hoop is made of plastic, 31-35" in diameter. The equipment is small in size to fit the younger gymnasts.

Natali did rolls, high tosses, catches, spins and passes through the hoop.

The clubs are made of plastic and are equal in length. Natali did various throws and catches requiring twice the precise timing because there are two of them.

She also created circles and mills. Mills are when the clubs swing opposite each other.

Persistent practice is what makes all of these maneuvers possible.

Natali was improving everyday and just in time for the Mini-Olympics, an annual event held by the gym for the gymnasts to perform for family and friends.

The higher level rhythmic team came out with their ribbons dancing in the air, an amazing spectacle of color and movement.

At the end of the rhythmic performance, Tina asked one of the younger girls, Katy to perform her ball routine. Katy was very flexible and a promising rhythmic gymnast. She did her routine perfectly and everyone applauded.

Natali, standing on the side watching, suddenly turned to Tina and asked to perform her rope routine. Tina, who was surprised, said, "Yes."

So eight year old Natali picked up her rope and walked alone confidently to the middle of the floor. She jumped and leaped under and over the rope in time with the music. Everyone was amazed including her parents. After her ending pose, she smiled and saluted. She and Katy both got awards.

Natali was ready for competition.

In 2001, Natali won a Junior Olympic National Championship.

Her hard work and love for the sport helped her continue on to win medals for the next five years.

*Dedicated to my daughter Mandy who inspires and amazes us always and to the coaches at Westside Gymastics Academy: Bettina Megowan, Wuling Stephenson and in loving memory of Irina Gabashvili.*

*Thanks to Ted Kukula who has helped make all of this possible.*

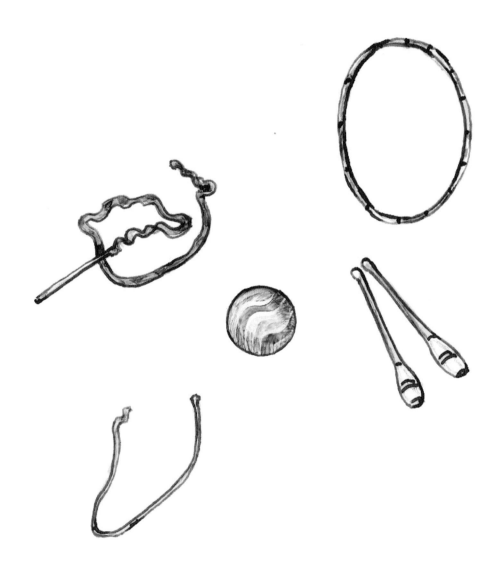

Made in the USA
Lexington, KY
02 December 2012